SUPER EASY SONGBOOK

ED SHEERAN

T0068384

Cover photo © Getty Images / Taylor Hill / Contributor

ISBN 978-1-5400-4315-3

Visit Hal Leonard Online at
www.halleonard.com

Contact us:
Hal Leonard
7777 West Bluemound Road
Milwaukee, WI 53213
Email: info@halleonard.com

In Europe, contact:
Hal Leonard Europe Limited
42 Wigmore Street
Marylebone, London, W1U 2RN
Email: info@halleonardeurope.com

In Australia, contact:
Hal Leonard Australia Pty. Ltd.
4 Lentara Court
Cheltenham, Victoria, 3192 Australia
Email: info@halleonard.com.au

Welcome to the *Super Easy Songbook* series!

This unique collection will help you play your favorite songs quickly and easily. Here's how it works:

- Play the simplified melody with your right hand. Letter names appear inside each note to assist you.

- There are no key signatures to worry about! If a sharp ♯ or flat ♭ is needed, it is shown beside the note each time.

- There are no page turns, so your hands never have to leave the keyboard.

- If two notes are connected by a tie ⌣, hold the first note for the combined number of beats. (The second note does not show a letter name since it is not re-struck.)

- Add basic chords with your left hand using the provided keyboard diagrams. Chord voicings have been carefully chosen to minimize hand movement.

- The left-hand rhythm is up to you, and chord notes can be played together or separately. Be creative!

- If the chords sound muddy, move your left hand an octave* higher. If this gets in the way of playing the melody, move your right hand an octave higher as well.

   * *An octave spans eight notes. If your starting note is C, the next C to the right is an octave higher.*

—————————————— ALSO AVAILABLE ——————————————

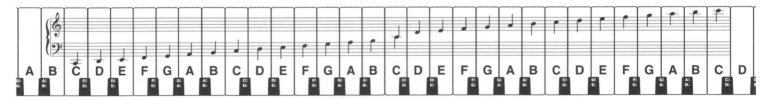

Hal Leonard Student Keyboard Guide HL00296039

Key Stickers HL00100016

The A Team

G Em Am C D

Words and Music by
Ed Sheeran

Moderately

White lips, pale face, breath-ing in snow-flakes. Burnt lungs, sour

taste. Light's gone, day's end. Strug-gl-ing to pay

rent. Long nights, strange men. And they say she's in the Class

A team. Stuck in her day-dream. Been this way since eight-een, but late-ly her

face seems slow-ly sink-ing, wast-ing, crum-bl-ing like

pas - tries. And they scream: the worst things in life come free to us, 'cause we're

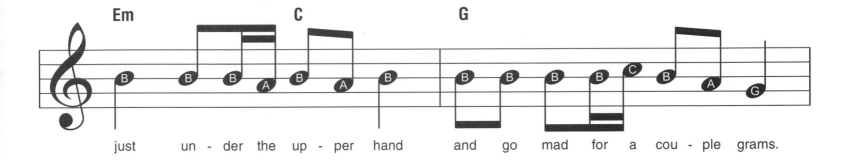

just un - der the up - per hand and go mad for a cou - ple grams.

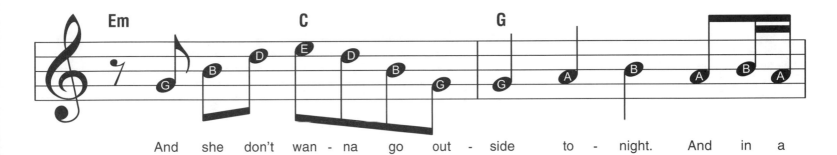

And she don't wan - na go out - side to - night. And in a

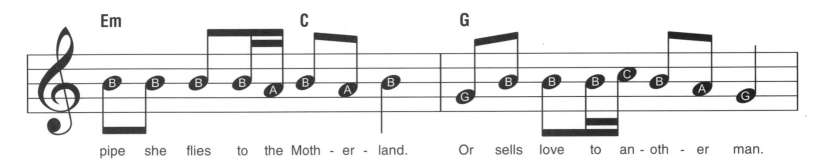

pipe she flies to the Moth - er - land. Or sells love to an - oth - er man.

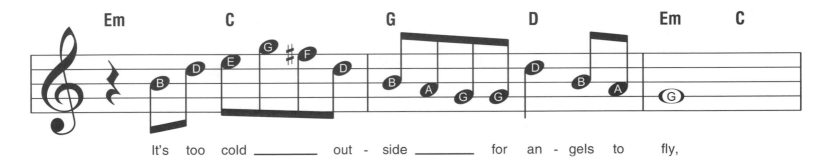

It's too cold _____ out - side _____ for an - gels to fly,

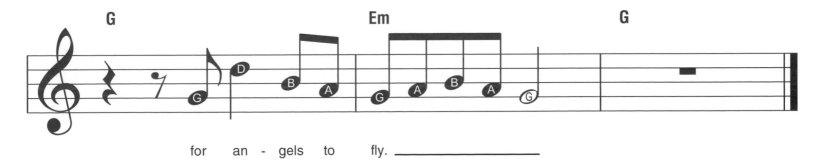

for an - gels to fly. _____

All of the Stars

from the Motion Picture Soundtrack THE FAULT IN OUR STARS

Bloodstream

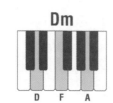 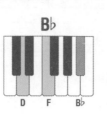 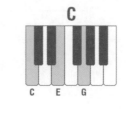 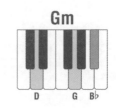

Words and Music by Ed Sheeran,
Amir Izadkhah, Kesi Dryden,
Piers Aggett, John McDaid
and Gary Lightbody

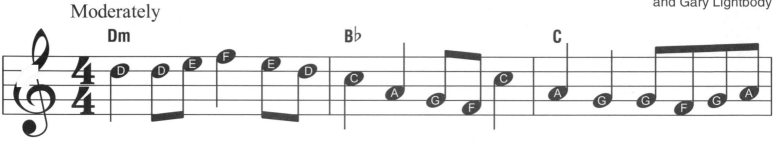

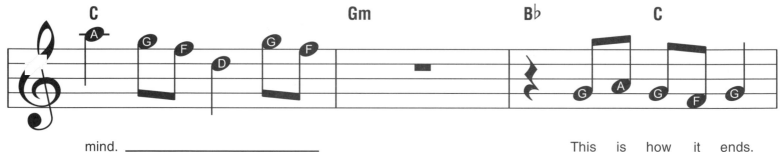

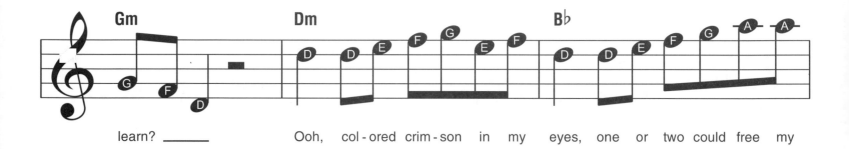

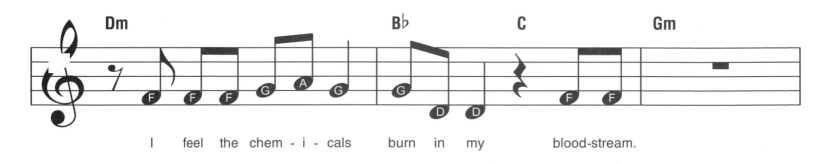

11

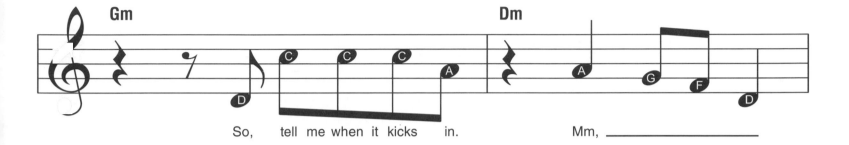

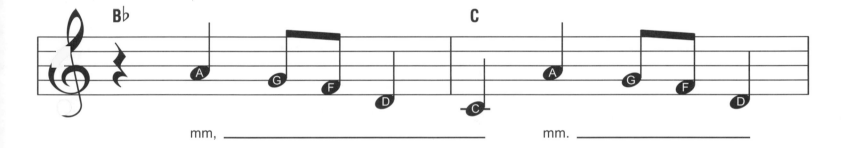

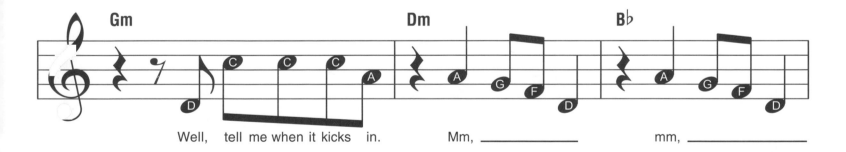

Castle on the Hill

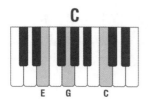
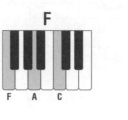
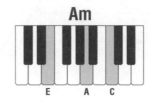
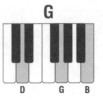

Words and Music by Ed Sheeran
and Benjamin Levin

Moderately fast

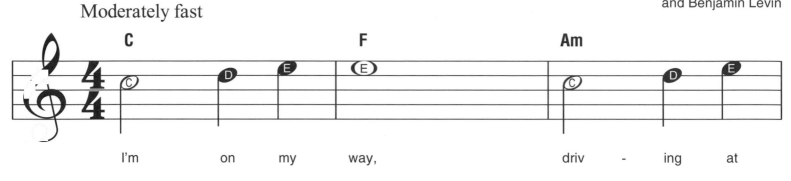

I'm on my way, driv - ing at

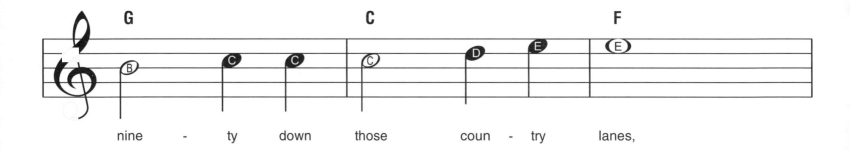

nine - ty down those coun - try lanes,

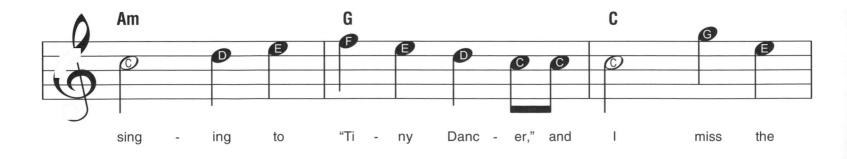

sing - ing to "Ti - ny Danc - er," and I miss the

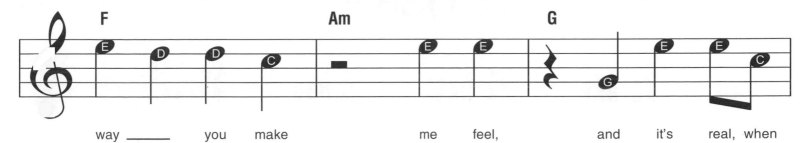

way _____ you make me feel, and it's real, when

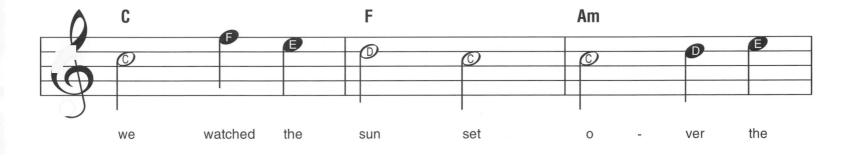

we watched the sun set o - ver the

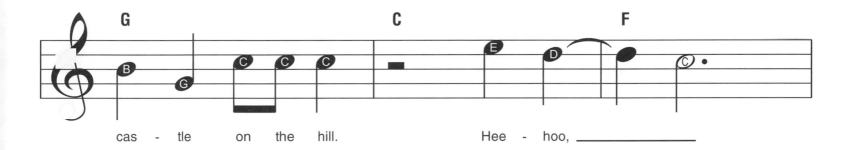

cas - tle on the hill. Hee - hoo, _____

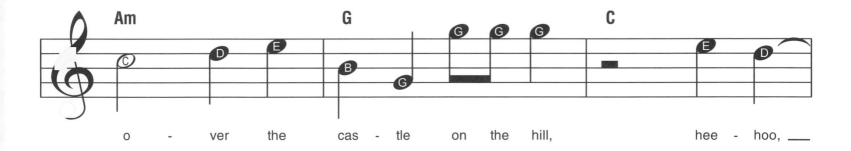

o - ver the cas - tle on the hill, hee - hoo, ___

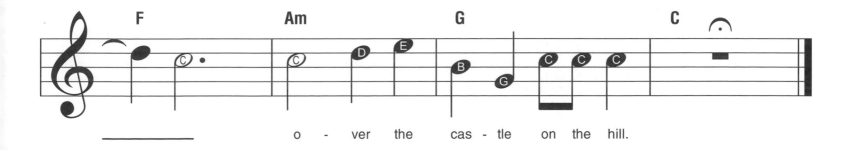

_____ o - ver the cas - tle on the hill.

Don't

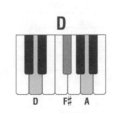

Words and Music by Ed Sheeran,
Dawn Robinson, Benjamin Levin,
Raphael Saadiq, Ali Jones-Muhammad
and Conesha Owens

Moderately fast
(no chord)

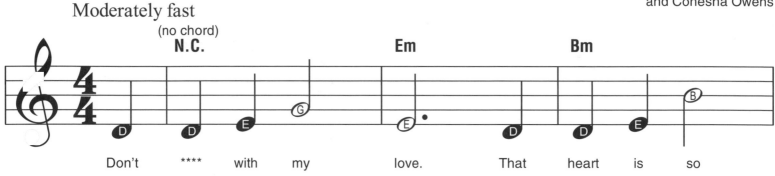

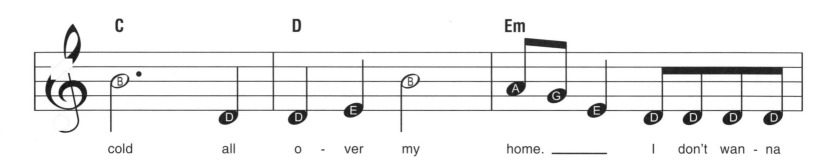

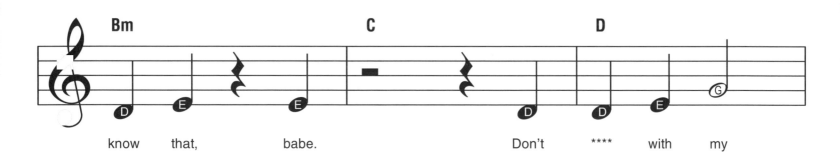

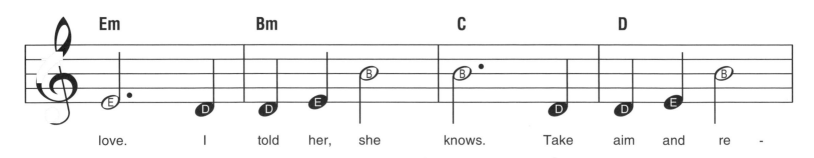

15

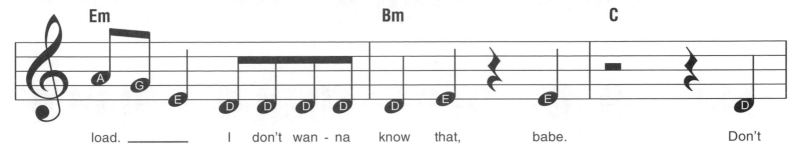

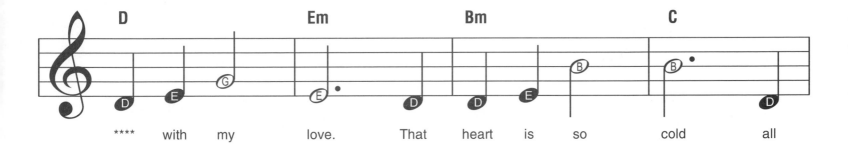

load. _____ I don't wan - na know that, babe. Don't

**** with my love. That heart is so cold all

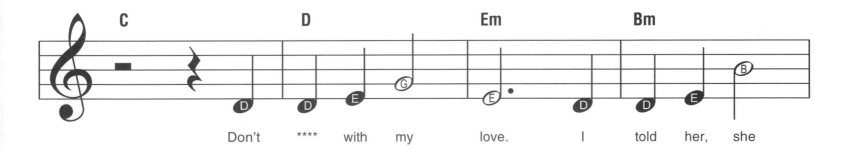

o - ver my home. _____ I don't wanna know that, babe.

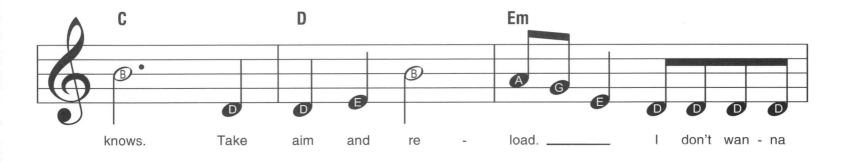

Don't **** with my love. I told her, she

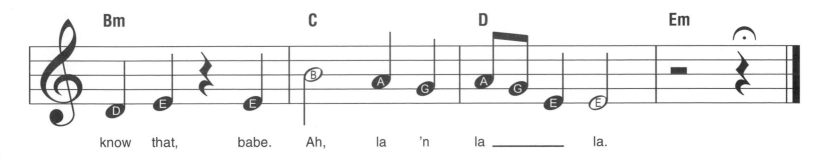

knows. Take aim and re - load. _____ I don't wan - na

know that, babe. Ah, la 'n la _____ la.

Drunk

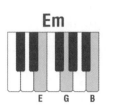
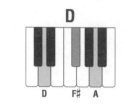
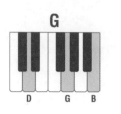
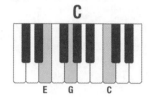
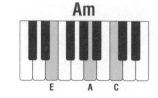

Words and Music by Ed Sheeran
and Jake Gosling

Moderately fast

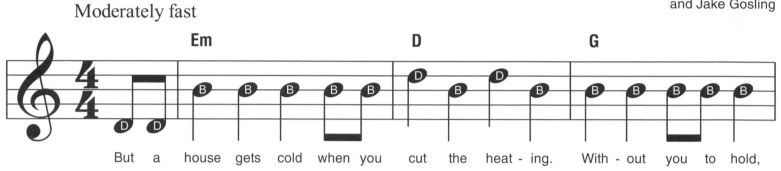

But a house gets cold when you cut the heat - ing. With - out you to hold,

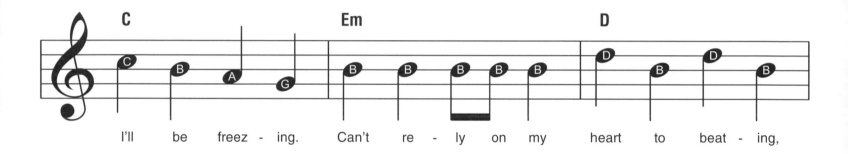

I'll be freez - ing. Can't re - ly on my heart to beat - ing,

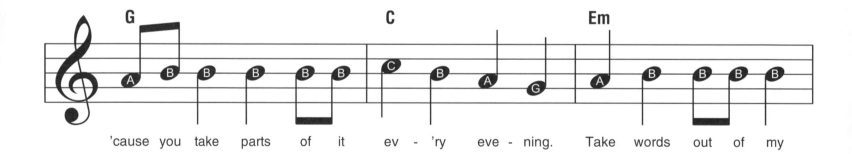

'cause you take parts of it ev - 'ry eve - ning. Take words out of my

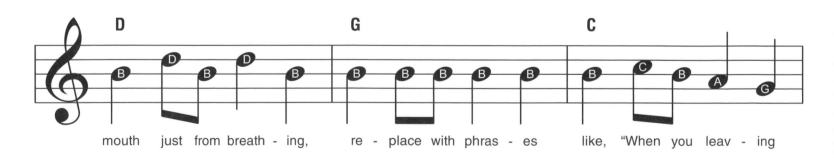

mouth just from breath - ing, re - place with phras - es like, "When you leav - ing

17

me?"   Should I?   Should I?

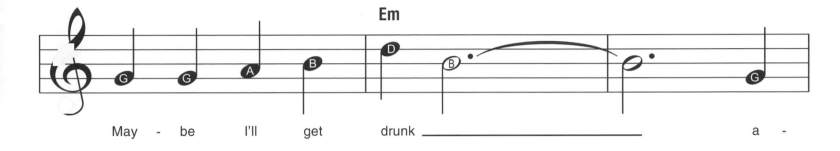

May - be   I'll   get   drunk _____   a -

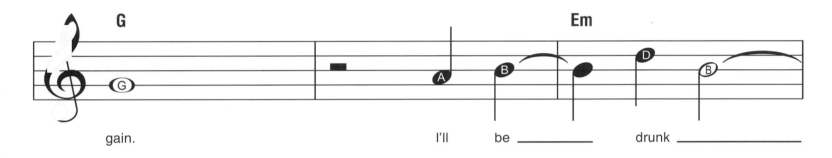

gain.   I'll   be _____   drunk _____

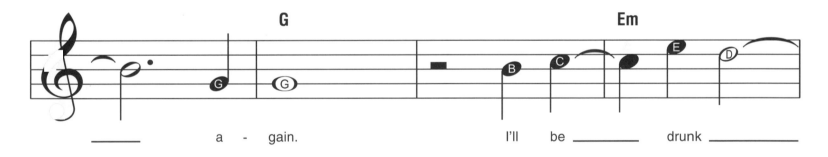

_____   a - gain.   I'll   be _____   drunk _____

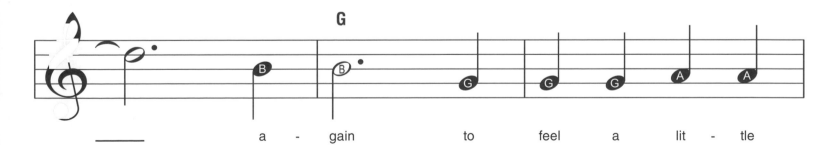

_____   a - gain   to   feel   a   lit - tle

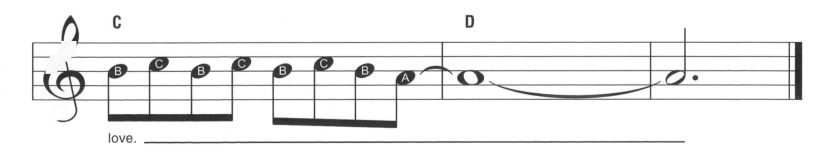

love. _____

Galway Girl

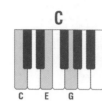
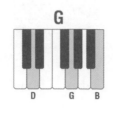
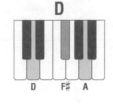
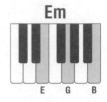

Words and Music by Ed Sheeran,
Foy Vance, John McDaid,
Amy Wadge, Eamon Murray,
Niamh Dunne, Liam Bradley,
Damian McKee and Sean Graham

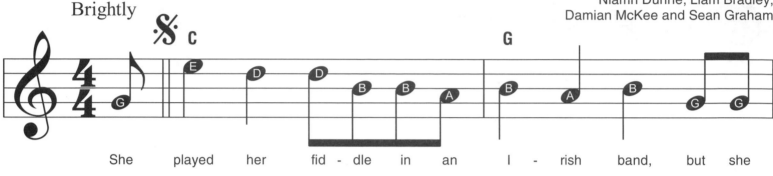

She played her fid - dle in an I - rish band, but she

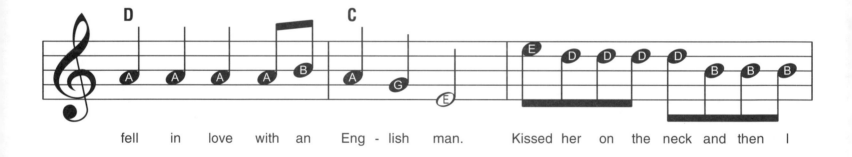

fell in love with an Eng - lish man. Kissed her on the neck and then I

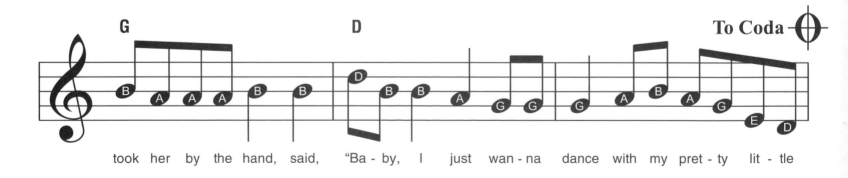

took her by the hand, said, "Ba - by, I just wan - na dance with my pret - ty lit - tle

Give Me Love

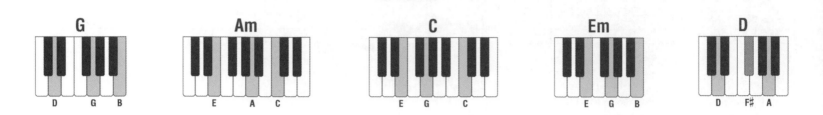

Words and Music by Ed Sheeran,
Chris Leonard and Jake Gosling

Moderately fast

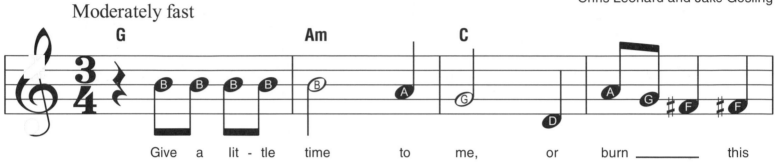

Give a lit - tle time to me, or burn _____ this

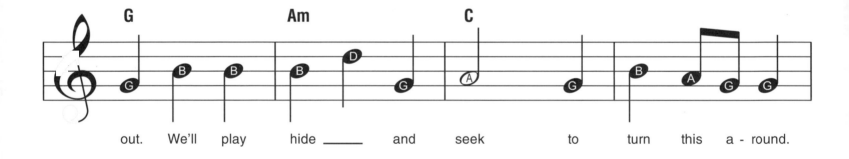

out. We'll play hide _____ and seek to turn this a - round.

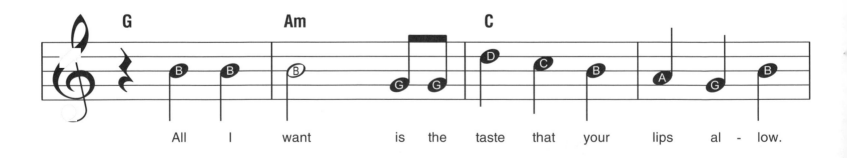

All I want is the taste that your lips al - low.

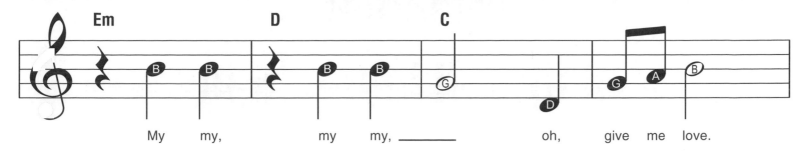

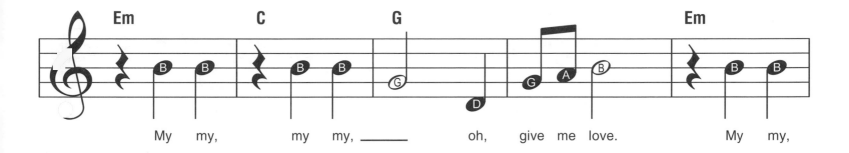

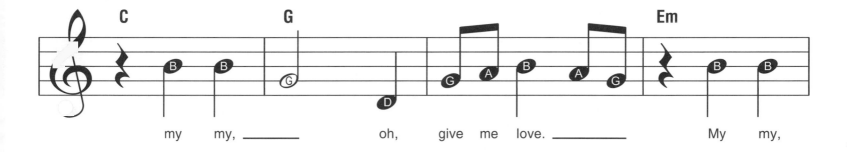

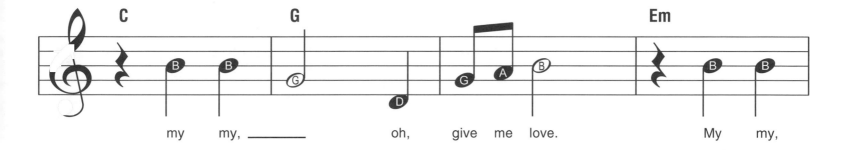

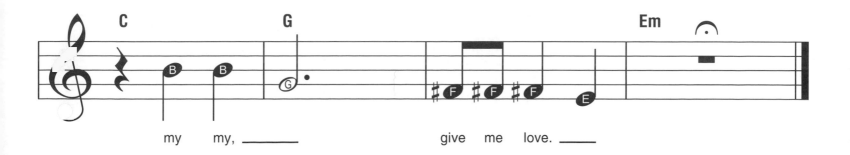

Happier

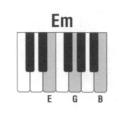
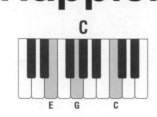
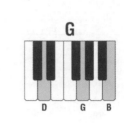

Words and Music by Ed Sheeran,
Benjamin Levin and Ryan Tedder

23

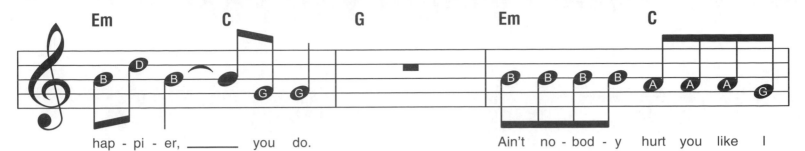

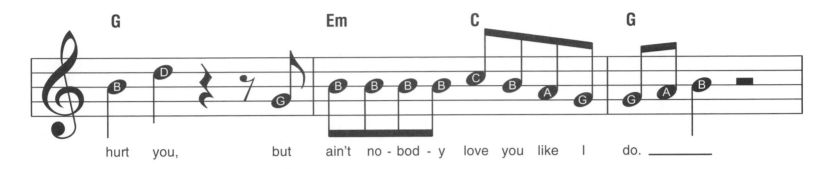

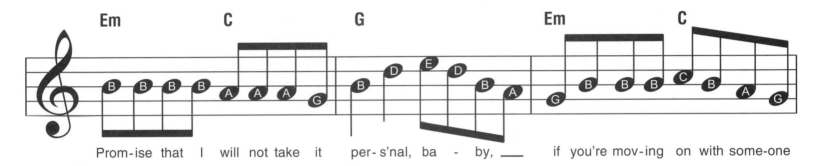

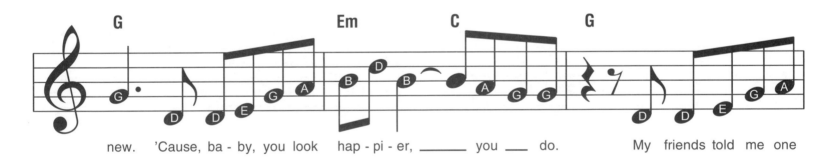

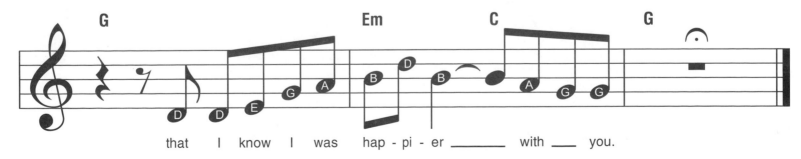

How Would You Feel
(Paean)

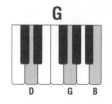
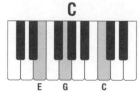
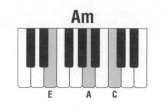
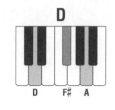

Words and Music by
Ed Sheeran

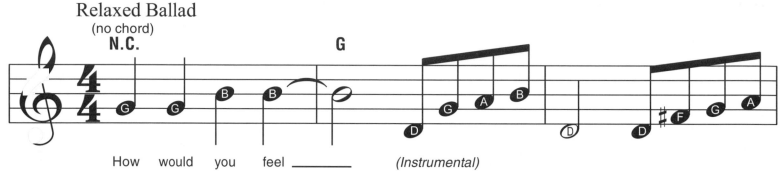

How would you feel _____ (Instrumental)

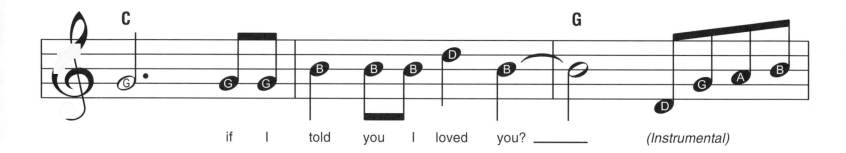

if I told you I loved you? _____ (Instrumental)

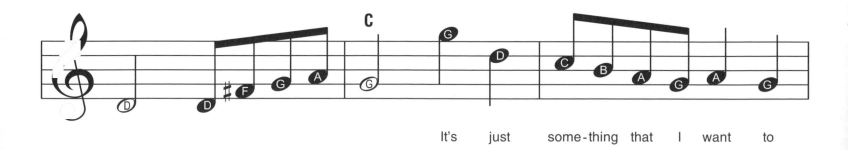

It's just some-thing that I want to

do. *(Instrumental)* I'll be

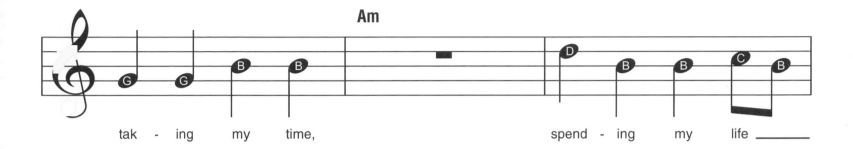

tak - ing my time, spend - ing my life _____

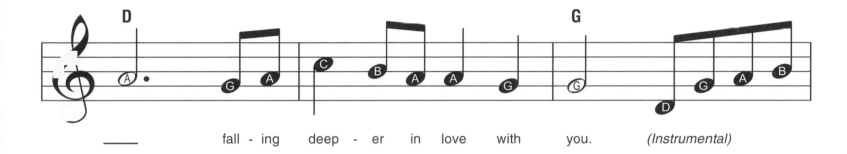

_____ fall - ing deep - er in love with you. *(Instrumental)*

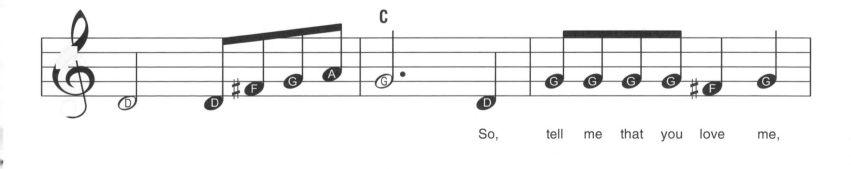

So, tell me that you love me,

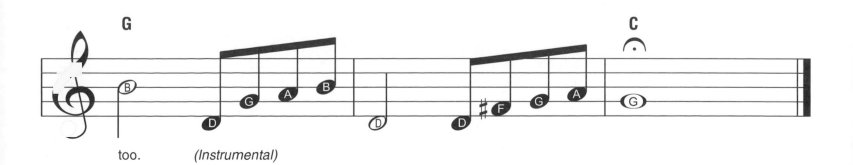

too. *(Instrumental)*

I See Fire

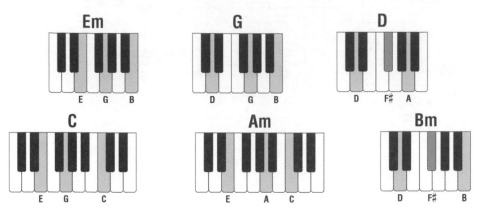

Words and Music by
Ed Sheeran

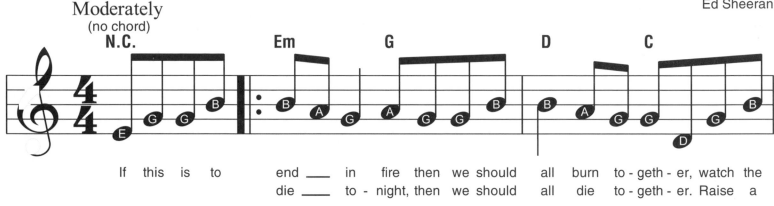

Moderately
(no chord)

If this is to end ___ in fire then we should all burn to-geth-er, watch the
die ___ to-night, then we should all die to-geth-er. Raise a

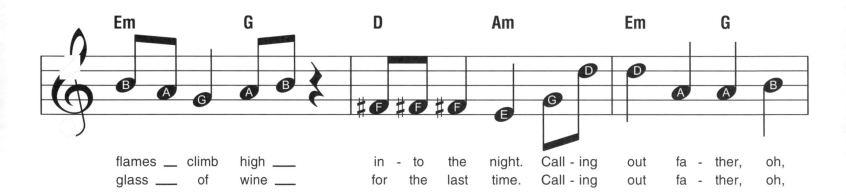

flames ___ climb high ___ in-to the night. Call-ing out fa-ther, oh,
glass ___ of wine ___ for the last time. Call-ing out fa-ther, oh,

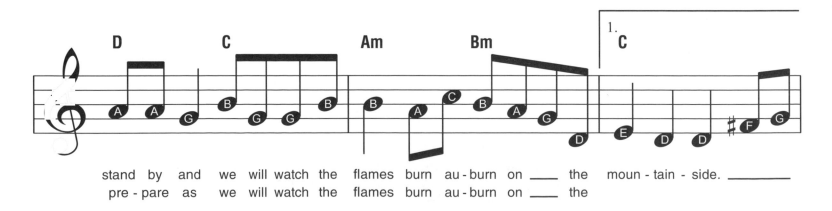

stand by and we will watch the flames burn au-burn on ___ the moun-tain-side. ___
pre-pare as we will watch the flames burn au-burn on ___ the

27

And if we should moun - tain - side. Des - o -

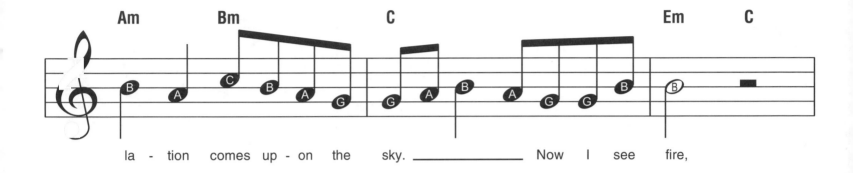

la - tion comes up - on the sky. _____ Now I see fire,

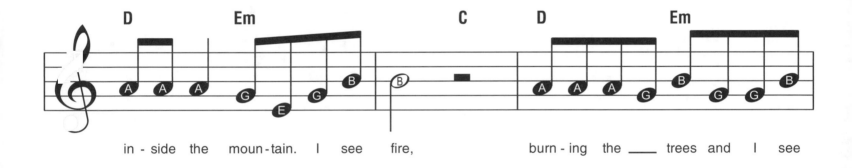

in - side the moun - tain. I see fire, burn - ing the ___ trees and I see

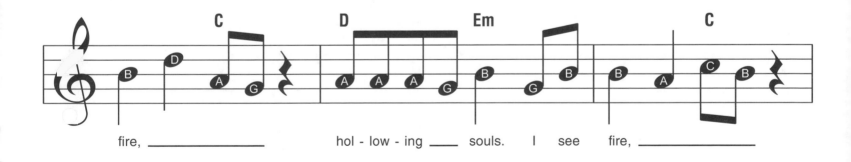

fire, _____ hol - low - ing ___ souls. I see fire, _____

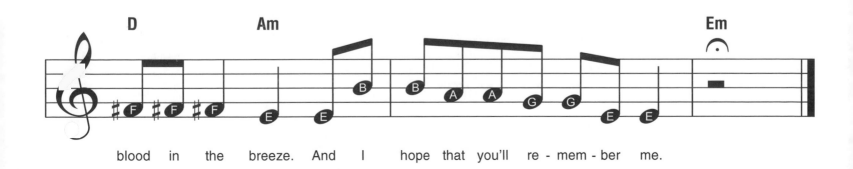

blood in the breeze. And I hope that you'll re - mem - ber me.

I'm a Mess

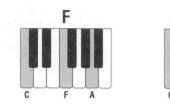
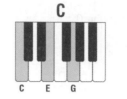
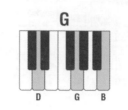
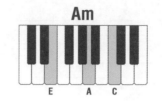

Words and Music by
Ed Sheeran

Moderately fast

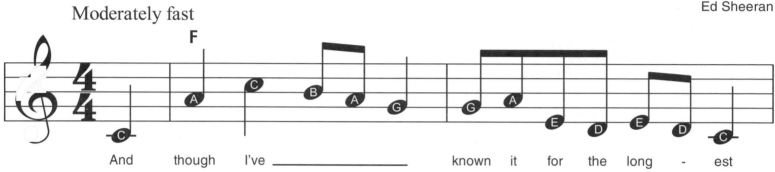

And though I've _____ known it for the long - est

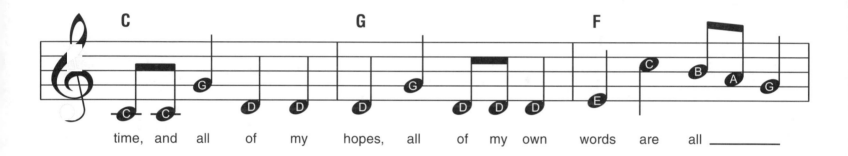

time, and all of my hopes, all of my own words are all _____

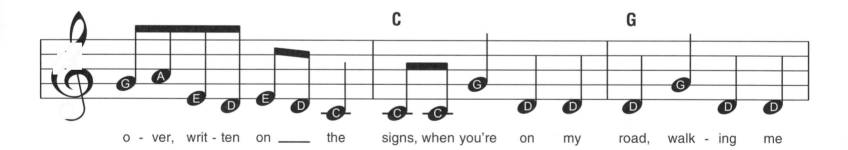

o - ver, writ - ten on ___ the signs, when you're on my road, walk - ing me

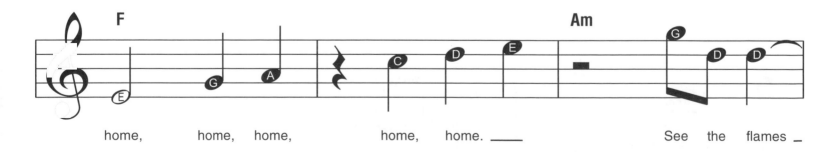

home, home, home, home, home. ____ See the flames _

29

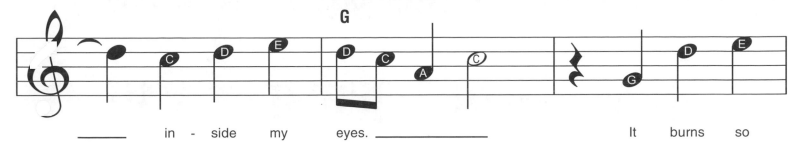

in - side my eyes. _____ It burns so

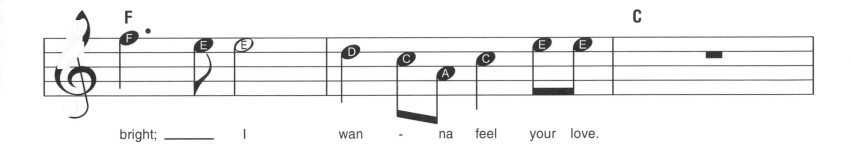

bright; _____ I wan - na feel your love.

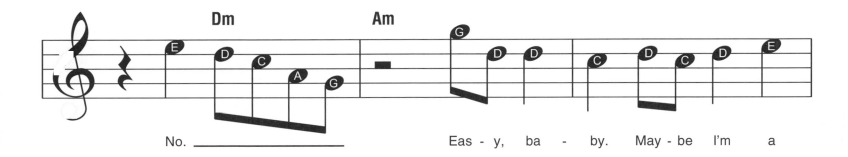

No. _____ Eas - y, ba - by. May - be I'm a

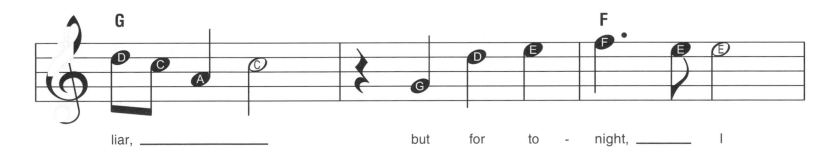

liar, _____ but for to - night, _____ I

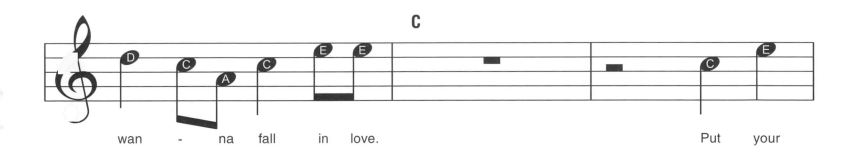

wan - na fall in love. Put your

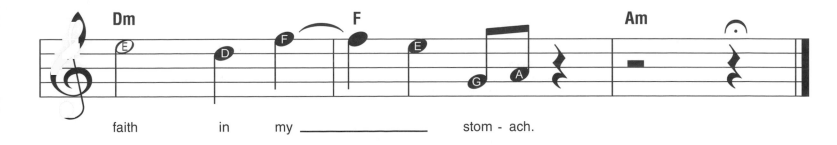

faith in my _____ stom - ach.

Kiss Me

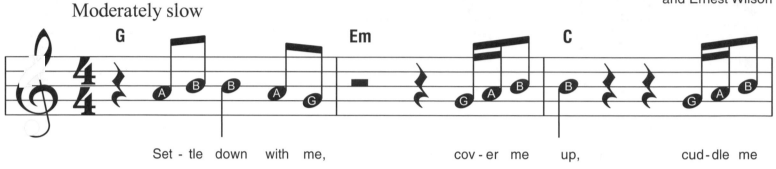

Words and Music by Ed Sheeran,
Julie Frost, Justin Franks
and Ernest Wilson

Moderately slow

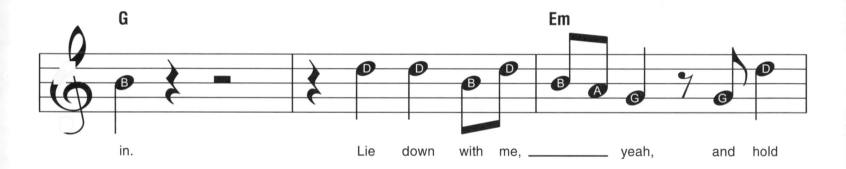

Set - tle down with me, cov - er me up, cud - dle me in. Lie down with me, _____ yeah, and hold

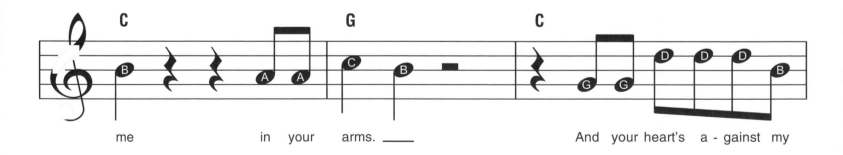

me in your arms. ____ And your heart's a - gainst my

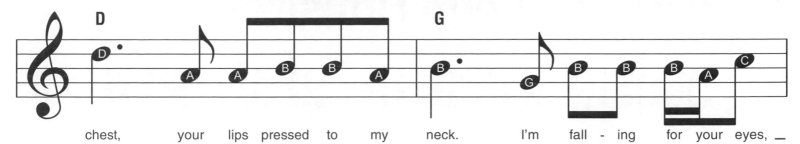

chest, your lips pressed to my neck. I'm fall - ing for your eyes, __

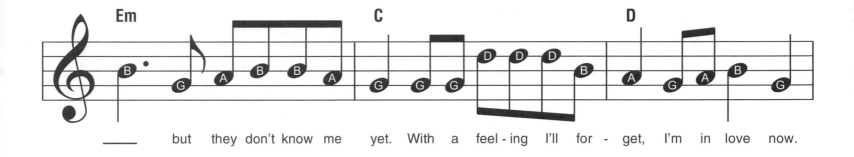

__ but they don't know me yet. With a feel - ing I'll for - get, I'm in love now.

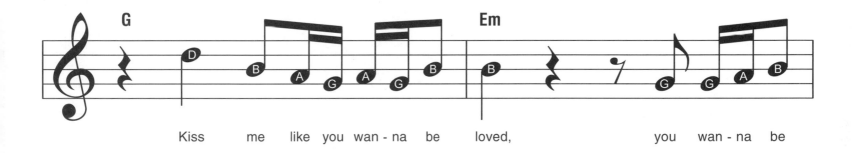

Kiss me like you wan - na be loved, you wan - na be

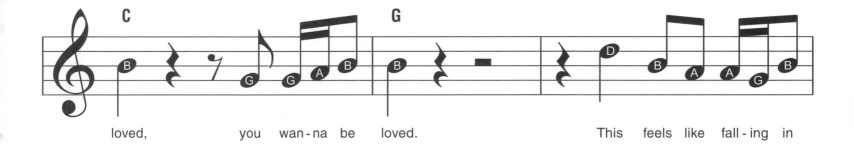

loved, you wan - na be loved. This feels like fall - ing in

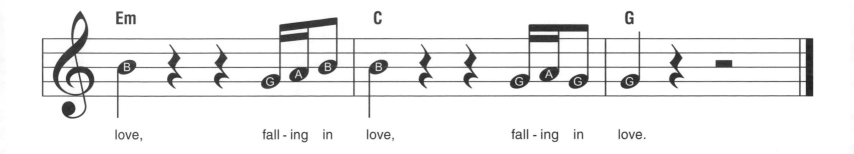

love, fall - ing in love, fall - ing in love.

Lego House

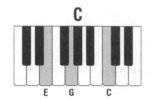

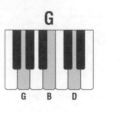
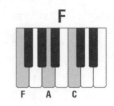

Words and Music by Ed Sheeran,
Chris Leonard and Jake Gosling

Moderately fast

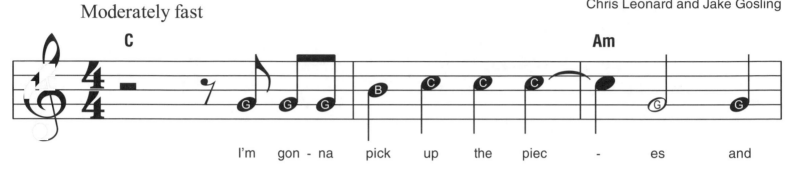

I'm gon-na pick up the piec - es and

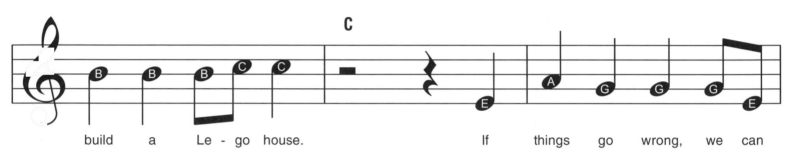

build a Le-go house. If things go wrong, we can

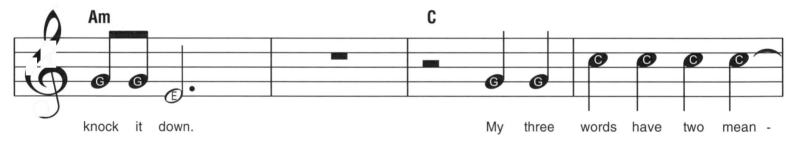

knock it down. My three words have two mean -

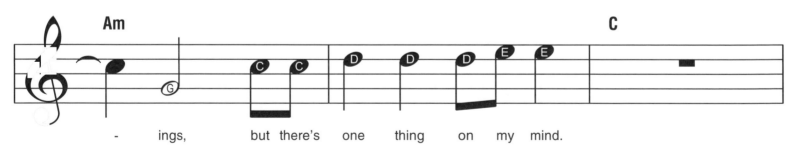

- ings, but there's one thing on my mind.

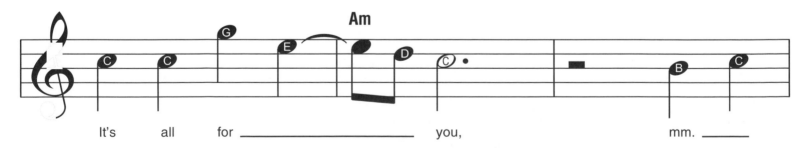

It's all for _____ you, mm. _____

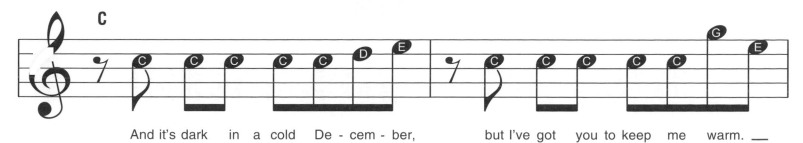

And it's dark in a cold De - cem - ber, but I've got you to keep me warm. __

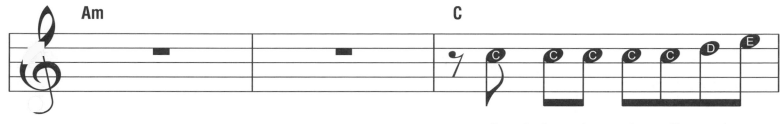

If you're bro - ken, I will mend ya,

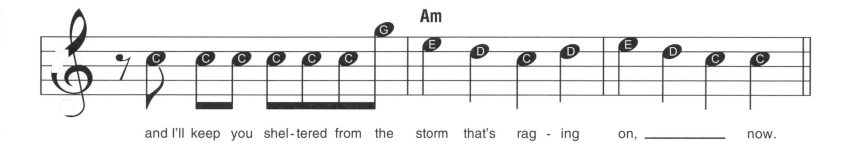

and I'll keep you shel - tered from the storm that's rag - ing on, _____ now.

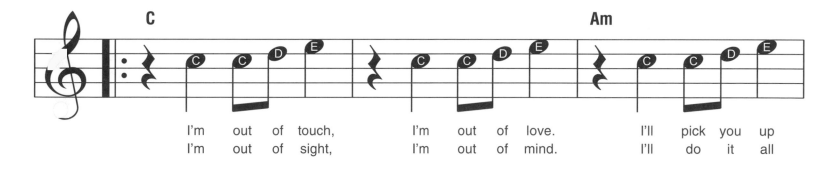

I'm out of touch, I'm out of love. I'll pick you up
I'm out of sight, I'm out of mind. I'll do it all

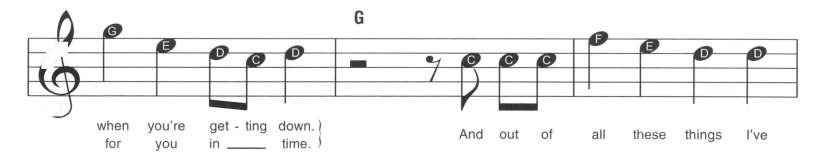

when you're get - ting down. }
for you in _____ time. }

And out of all these things I've

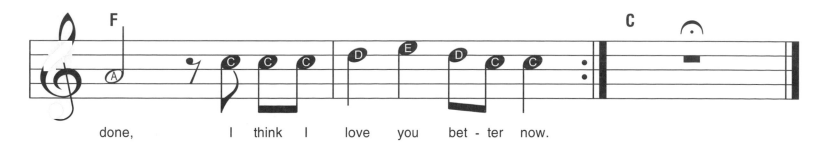

done, I think I love you bet - ter now.

Perfect

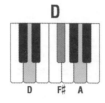
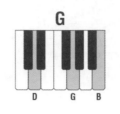
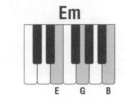
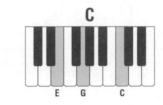

Words and Music by
Ed Sheeran

I'm danc - ing in the dark _____ with

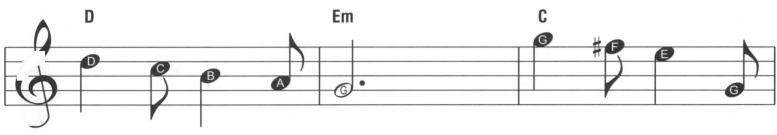

you be - tween my arms. Bare - foot on the

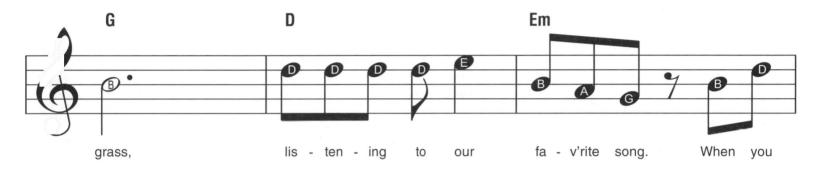

grass, lis - ten - ing to our fa - v'rite song. When you

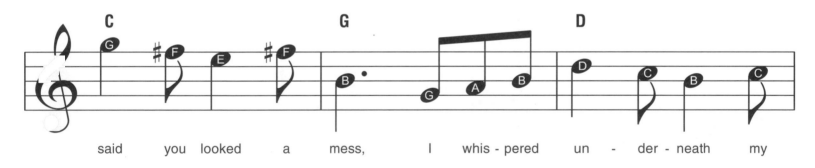

said you looked a mess, I whis - pered un - der - neath my

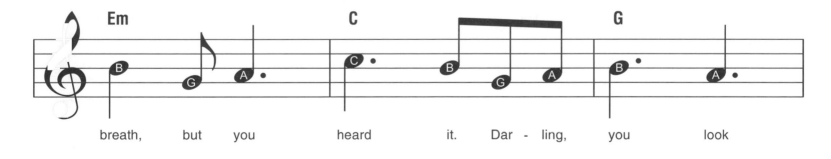

breath, but you heard it. Dar - ling, you look

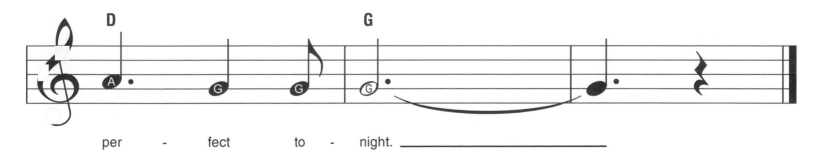

per - fect to - night. _____

Photograph

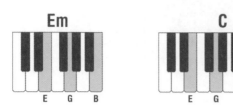
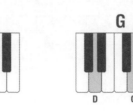
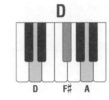

Words and Music by Ed Sheeran,
Johnny McDaid, Martin Peter Harrington
and Tom Leonard

Moderately

We keep this love in a pho - to - graph.

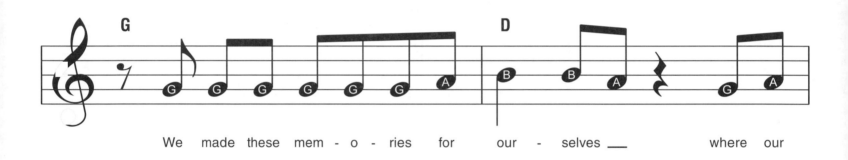

We made these mem - o - ries for our - selves ___ where our

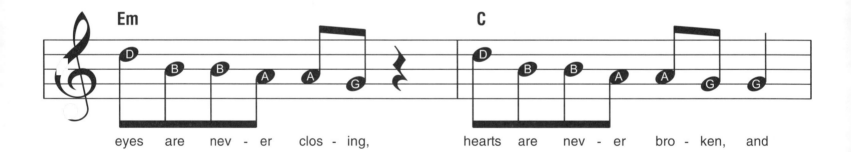

eyes are nev - er clos - ing,   hearts are nev - er bro - ken, and

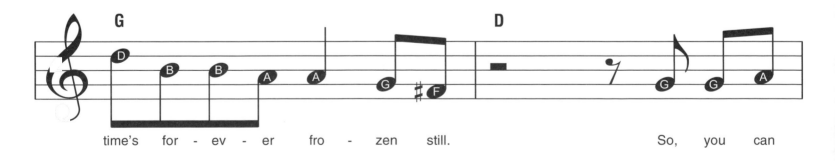

time's for - ev - er fro - zen still.   So, you can

Shape of You

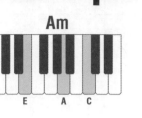
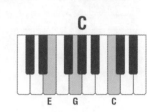
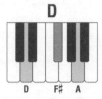

Words and Music by Ed Sheeran,
Kevin Briggs, Kandi Burruss,
Tameka Cottle, Steve Mac
and Johnny McDaid

Girl, you know I want your love. Your love was hand - made
"Boy, _____ let's not talk too much. Grab on my waist and

for some - bod - y like me. Come on, now, fol - low my lead.
put that bod - y on me." Come on, now,

I may be cra - zy, don't mind me. Say, fol - low my lead. Come,

come on, now, fol - low my lead. Mmm. _____ I'm in love with the shape of

Sing

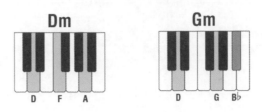

Words and Music by Ed Sheeran
and Pharrell Williams

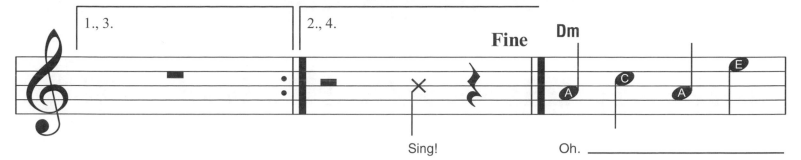

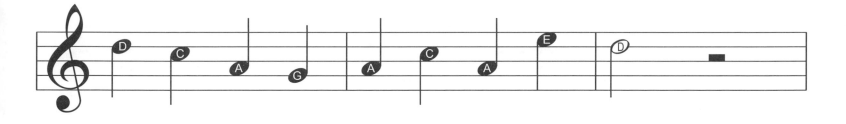

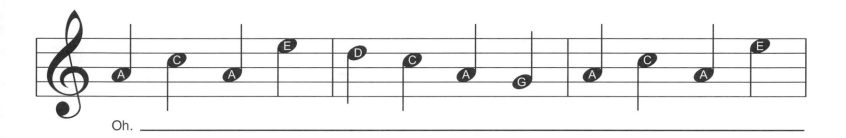

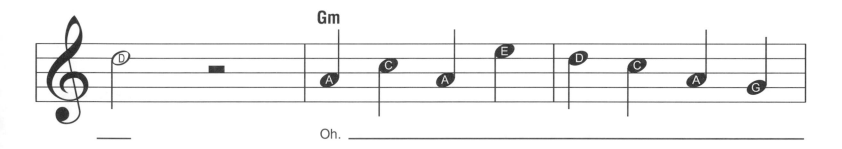

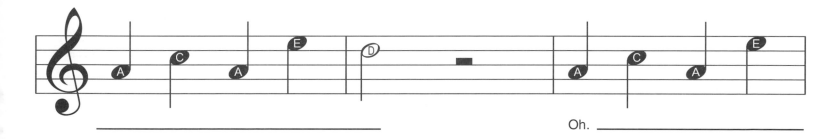

Tenerife Sea

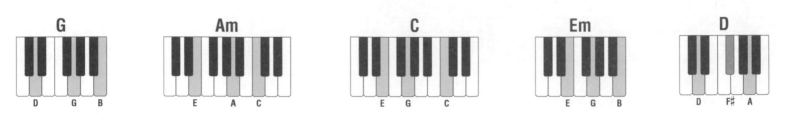

Words and Music by Ed Sheeran,
John McDaid and Foy Vance

Flowing

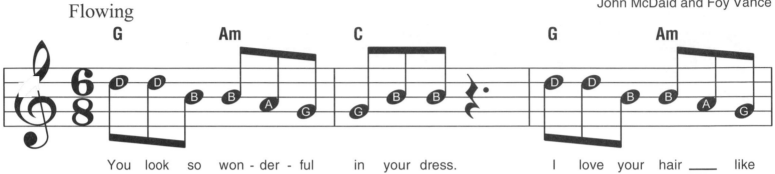

You look so won-der-ful in your dress. I love your hair ___ like

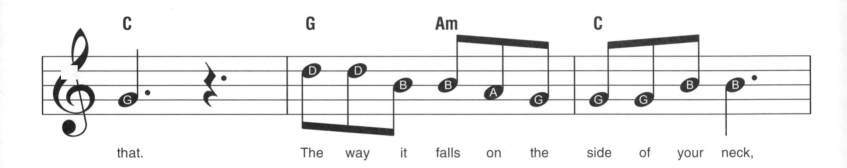

that. The way it falls on the side of your neck,

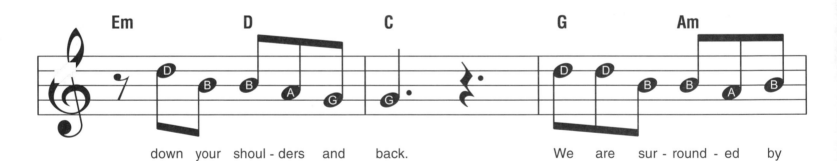

down your shoul-ders and back. We are sur-round-ed by

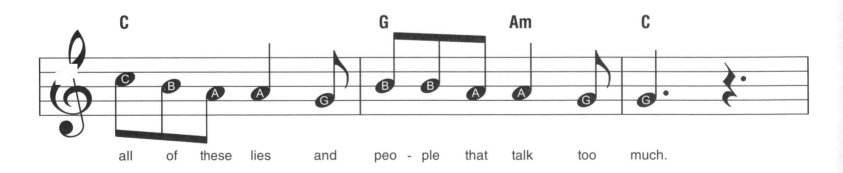

all of these lies and peo-ple that talk too much.

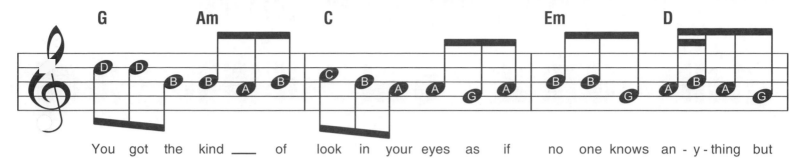

You got the kind ___ of look in your eyes as if no one knows an - y - thing but

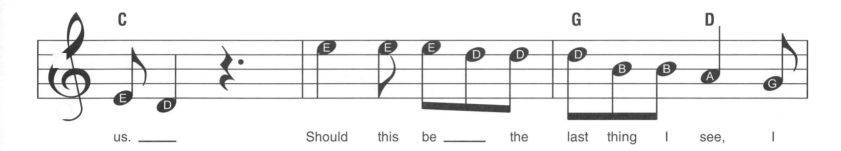

us. _____ Should this be _____ the last thing I see, I

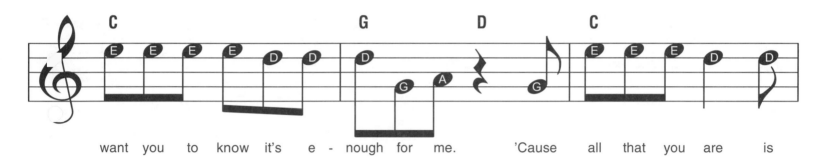

want you to know it's e - nough for me. 'Cause all that you are is

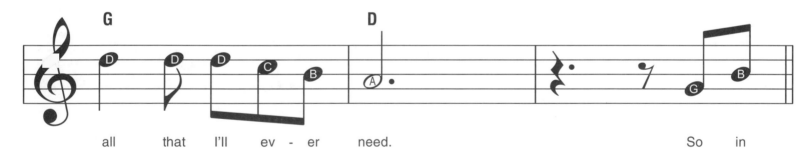

all that I'll ev - er need. So in

love, so in love.

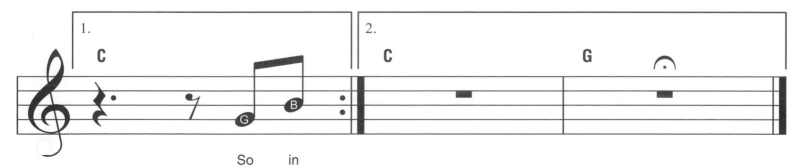

1.

2.

So in

Thinking Out Loud

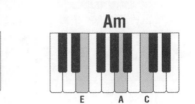

Words and Music by Ed Sheeran
and Amy Wadge

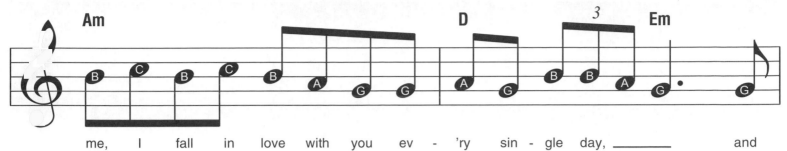

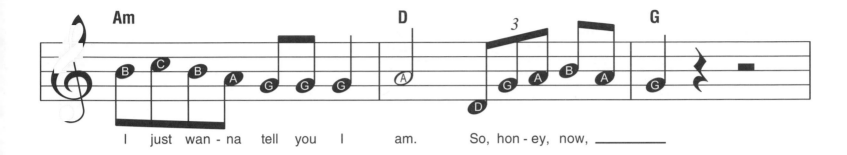

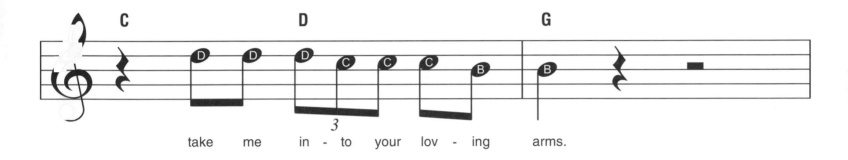

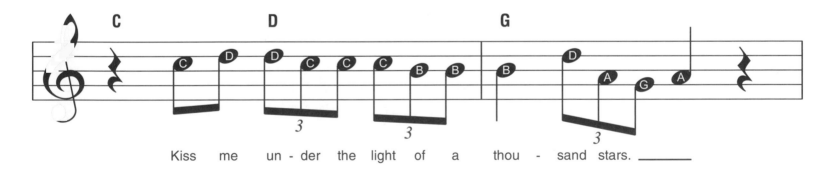

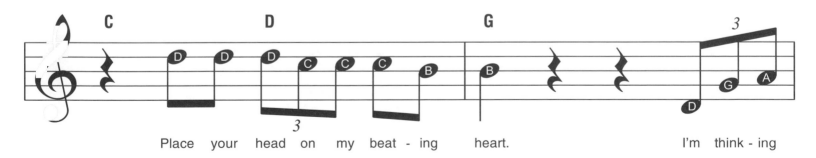

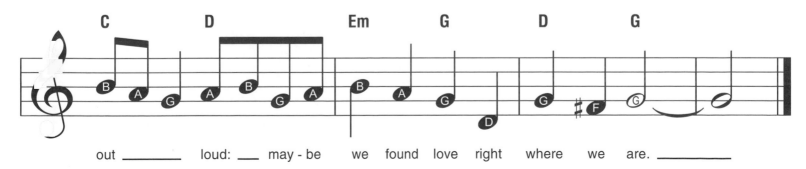

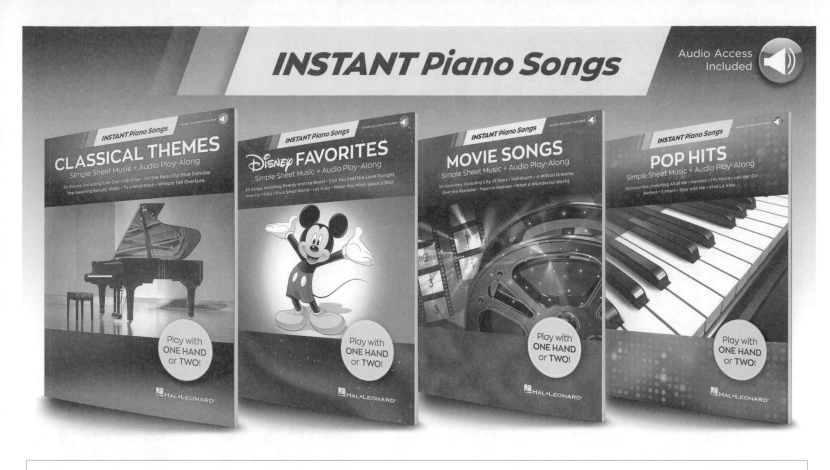

INSTANT Piano Songs

Audio Access Included

The **Instant Piano Songs** series will help you play your favorite songs quickly and easily—whether you use one hand or two! Start with the melody in your right hand, adding basic left-hand chords when you're ready. Letter names inside each note speed up the learning process, and optional rhythm patterns take your playing to the next level. Online backing tracks are also included. Stream or download the tracks using the unique code inside each book, then play along to build confidence and sound great!

CLASSICAL THEMES

Air (from *Water Music*) (Handel) • Can Can (Offenbach) • Canon (Pachelbel) • Danube Waves (Ivanovici) • Funeral March of a Marionette (Gounod) • Für Elise (Beethoven) • Impromptu, Op. 142, No. 2 (Schubert) • Jesu, Joy of Man's Desiring (Bach) • Jupiter (Holst) • Lullaby (Brahms) • The Merry Widow Waltz (Lehár) • Minuet I (Bach) • The Moldau (Smetana) • Musette (Bach) • On the Beautiful Blue Danube (Strauss) • Over the Waves (Rosas) • Pomp and Circumstance (Elgar) • Prelude, Op. 28, No. 7 (Chopin) • Rondeau (Mouret) • St. Anthony Chorale (Haydn) • The Sleeping Beauty Waltz (Tchaikovsky) • Sonata K. 331 (Mozart) • Spring (Vivaldi) • Spring Song (Mendelssohn) • Symphony No. 9, Second Movement ("From the New World") (Dvořák) • Symphony No. 9, Fourth Movement ("Ode to Joy") (Beethoven) • To a Wild Rose (MacDowell) • Trumpet Tune (Purcell) • Trumpet Voluntary (Clarke) • William Tell Overture (Rossini).
00283826 Easy Piano Solo $14.99

DISNEY FAVORITES

The Ballad of Davy Crockett • The Bare Necessities • Beauty and the Beast • Bibbidi-Bobbidi-Boo (The Magic Song) • Can You Feel the Love Tonight • Chim Chim Cher-ee • Circle of Life • Colors of the Wind • A Dream Is a Wish Your Heart Makes • Evermore • Friend like Me • God Help the Outcasts • How Does a Moment Last Forever • How Far I'll Go • I See the Light • If I Never Knew You (End Title) • It's a Small World • Kiss the Girl • Lava • Let It Go • Let's Go Fly a Kite • Mickey Mouse March • Part of Your World • Reflection • Remember Me (Ernesto de la Cruz) • Supercalifragilisticexpialidocious • That's How You Know • When She Loved Me • A Whole New World • You'll Be in My Heart (Pop Version).
00283720 Easy Piano Solo...$14.99

MOVIE SONGS

Alfie • As Time Goes By • The Candy Man • City of Stars • Days of Wine and Roses • Endless Love • Hallelujah • I Will Always Love You • Laura • A Million Dreams • Mrs. Robinson • Moon River • My Heart Will Go on (Love Theme from 'Titanic') • Theme from "New York, New York" • Over the Rainbow • Raindrops Keep Fallin' on My Head • Secret Love • Singin' in the Rain • Skyfall • Somewhere, My Love • Somewhere Out There • Stayin' Alive • Take My Breath Away (Love Theme) • Tears in Heaven • The Trolley Song • Unchained Melody • Up Where We Belong • The Way We Were • What a Wonderful World • Where Do I Begin (Love Theme).
00283718 Easy Piano Solo $14.99

POP HITS

All of Me • Can't Feel My Face • Chasing Cars • Despacito • Feel It Still • Happy • Havana • Hello • Hey, Soul Sister • Ho Hey • I Knew You Were Trouble • I'm Yours • Just Give Me a Reason • Let Her Go • Lost Boy • Love Yourself • Million Reasons • One Call Away • 100 Years • Perfect • Riptide • Say You Won't Let Go • See You Again • 7 Years • Shake It Off • Stay with Me • Thinking Out Loud • Viva La Vida • What Makes You Beautiful • You Are the Reason.
00283825 Easy Piano Solo $14.99

HAL•LEONARD®
www.halleonard.com

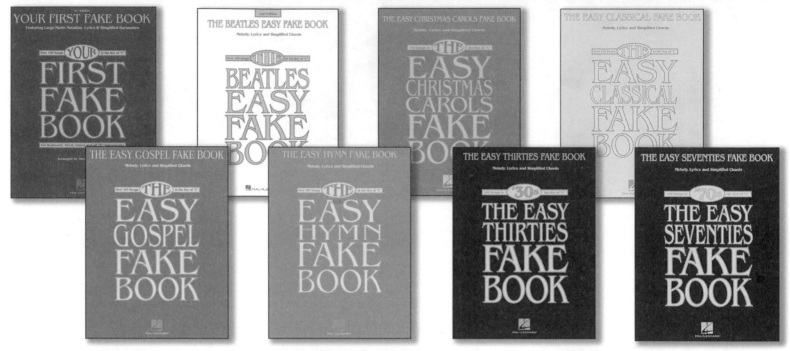